How to spot a Diamond Geezer

An essential Bubblegum guide

Ged Backland and Phil Renshaw

Diamond Geezer

Diamond Geezer is a top bloke. He's 100 per cent reliable and when a friend is in need, he is a friend indeed. He's got shoulders to laugh on, cry on and even flippin' sit on when you're having a mega laugh. An all round top bloke and proper friend. If you wanted someone to be there for you, then look no further than this diamond of a bloke.

Most Likely to Say... Do you need to talk?

Most Likely to Be... Helping an old git across the road

Fave Colour Diamond White

Bestest Friends with....
Sun Junkie
Footy Nut
Petrol Head

When Gym Queen exercises like mad
and gasps on the exercise bike
Diamond Geezer brings her some juice
'cos that's just what he's like!

Veggie likes to munch on leaves
so she joins Diamond for eats
'Cos Diamond's fridge is always full
of tasty veggie treats

When Drama Queen throws a wobbly
Diamond Geezer couldn't be calmer
'Cos he knows that this lass blows
small things up into a drama

So there you have it, now it's clear
The low-down on Diamond Geezer's here

If it all sounds familiar, if it all rings quite true
Then perhaps, well then just maybe,
That Diamond Geezer is you!